Diary
of
E.A.Provost

Private, do not read!

> **For Abby, Ellie,
> Maggie, & Winnie**
>
> My wonderful, fabulous, talented,
> and incredibly amazing daughters.
> Especially the editor.

First Edition
Produced by New Alexandria Creative Group
Sonoma County, California
Poetry & Art ©Copyright 2018 Elisabeth Provost
Follow the Author at www.themensamom.blogspot.com

Available via IngramSpark Print on Demand
wherever books are sold.
ISBN: 978-0-998137-1-3

Also avialable as an eBook through most outlets.
ISBN: 978-0-9998137-2-0

Cover: Self Portrait & Negative

It's my Poetry and I'll Rhyme if I want to.

As a child, I was encouraged to keep a diary, and given numerous beautiful blank, cloth covered volumes in which to do so, but I always felt my life far too boring to reflect upon daily. That hasn't changed, but in fourth grade I won a poetry contest at my school and discovered a new way to take pictures. Brilliant, four dimensional pictures that take shape within the reader's own brain, and convey the feeling of a moment rather than just the image. I began to write verse in those previously neglected journals. I carried one with me at all times. There are volumes of horrid poetry locked away in a chest in my garage; I won't bore you with a volume of my juvenilia.

I grew older, went to work, got married, and my writing waned. But something happened when I had children. There were moments I needed to record. Feelings I wanted to remember that my camera couldn't capture. I began to write again. And my verse had improved. All of that teenage nonsense amounted to a lot of practice. Some of my poems begged to be shared, and people wanted to hear them! People wanted to buy a book of them!! People who weren't even related to me!!!

My verse is still a reflection of my life. Not all of the things we think and feel are edifying or socially acceptable. I prefer to keep things light when I'm reciting. But I write both the light and the dark, and some of the dark is more beautiful and poignant than the light. So, I've held things back. It's not that I care if people disagree with me, I might disagree with me too when I've put a few more years behind me, but these poems were all my truth at the time, a snapshot of life at a particular moment, or in a particular season. I'm not in that moment anymore, so I can't argue about, or defend, what I felt or believed then. I can only hope that I write well enough for you to feel what I felt, and see what I saw, from where I once stood. I can only trust that you will appreciate this opportunity to sneak a peek in my diary, and pretend you didn't see anything naughty when you meet me after ;-).

The art in this collection is a selection of my work at Vertical Call over the last decade. It was painted during church worship services, and is often called Worship Art or Prophetic Art. I prefer to call it Encounter Art, as I encounter God at the canvas and it is my hope that others will as well.

Superstorm Winnie

Winnie is a whirlwind.
She'll blow you clean away.
Winnie is a hurricane,
That floods the tub today.

Winnie is an earthquake, eight points.
She'll shake you to your core.
Winnie sends a tidal wave,
Across the kitchen floor.

Winnie, great volcano god!
Erupting constantly.
Winnie moves like lava flows,
Steadily, straight to the sea.

Winnie zips like lightning bolts.
You can't capture the flash.
Winnie rolls like thunder does.
Did you hear something crash?

Yes, Winnie strikes like lightning,
Never in the same place twice.
Then smiles like the sunshine,
And you think she's awful nice.

When You Were Small

When you were small I held you and
    You snuggled in my arms.
I rocked you in my rocking chair
    And drank in all your charms.

I smelled the sweetness of your head
    And touched your little nose.
I couldn't put you in your bed
    Though peacefully you dozed.

The housework, patient, waited
    As I sat and rocked you there.
Long eyelashes on rosy cheeks,
    Pursed lips and fuzzy hair.

You breathed so softly sleeping,
    As my loving warmth you shared.
Your little fist gripped tight my shirt
    While I just rocked and stared.

The Dawdler

You were once a toddler
Who wandered here and there
Now you are a dawdler
Who wonders everywhere

I Promise

The world is very big
And I am very small
You call this a railing
But I call it a wall
I'd like to see much further
Than I can from way down here
Put me on your shoulders and
I won't pull on your ear…
Anymore.

Perspective

Toddle, wobble, roll, and twirl
Many ways to see the world.

Tummy, feet, head, knees, and rear
Know what I can see from here?

Birds, bugs, worms, and slugs
Mother, may I give them hugs?

Optimistic Child

I love the way you see the world;
The way you just don't care.
If other kids are being mean
You're simply unaware.

The whole world is your kingdom.
Within you reign supreme.
A place of love and happiness,
And on some days, ice cream.

Everyone you meet's a friend,
Your best friend for the day.
When this playtime is over it's
Ok that you can't stay.

For tomorrow comes so quickly.
As every daybreak does
And you expect another day
That supersedes what was.

As I sit and spy on you
I try to take your view.
My world becomes much better
When I see it as you do.

The Smart Kids' Excuse

I'm worried about the oceans,
About the land and trees.
Aliens crossing the border,
And also killer bees.
Eating so much junk food I get
Type 2 diabetes.

I worry about bugs and plants,
And Mommy poisoning the ants.
That people want to hurt us in
Afghanistan, and France.
Not being fast enough at school,
And peeing in my pants.

I'm worried about the Arctic,
Changes in the weather.
That I'm guilty of killing cows,
For hamburgers and leather.
And Mom and Dad, like other folks,
Won't just stay together.

I'm worried I could get cancer,
Or AIDS, or heart disease.
My eyeballs popping from my head,
If open when I sneeze.
And though homeless people scare me,
I don't want them to freeze.

I'm worried that kids are dying,
Both near and far away.
And about so many other things,
That I'm afraid to say.
I'm sorry, but my homework didn't
Seem important today.

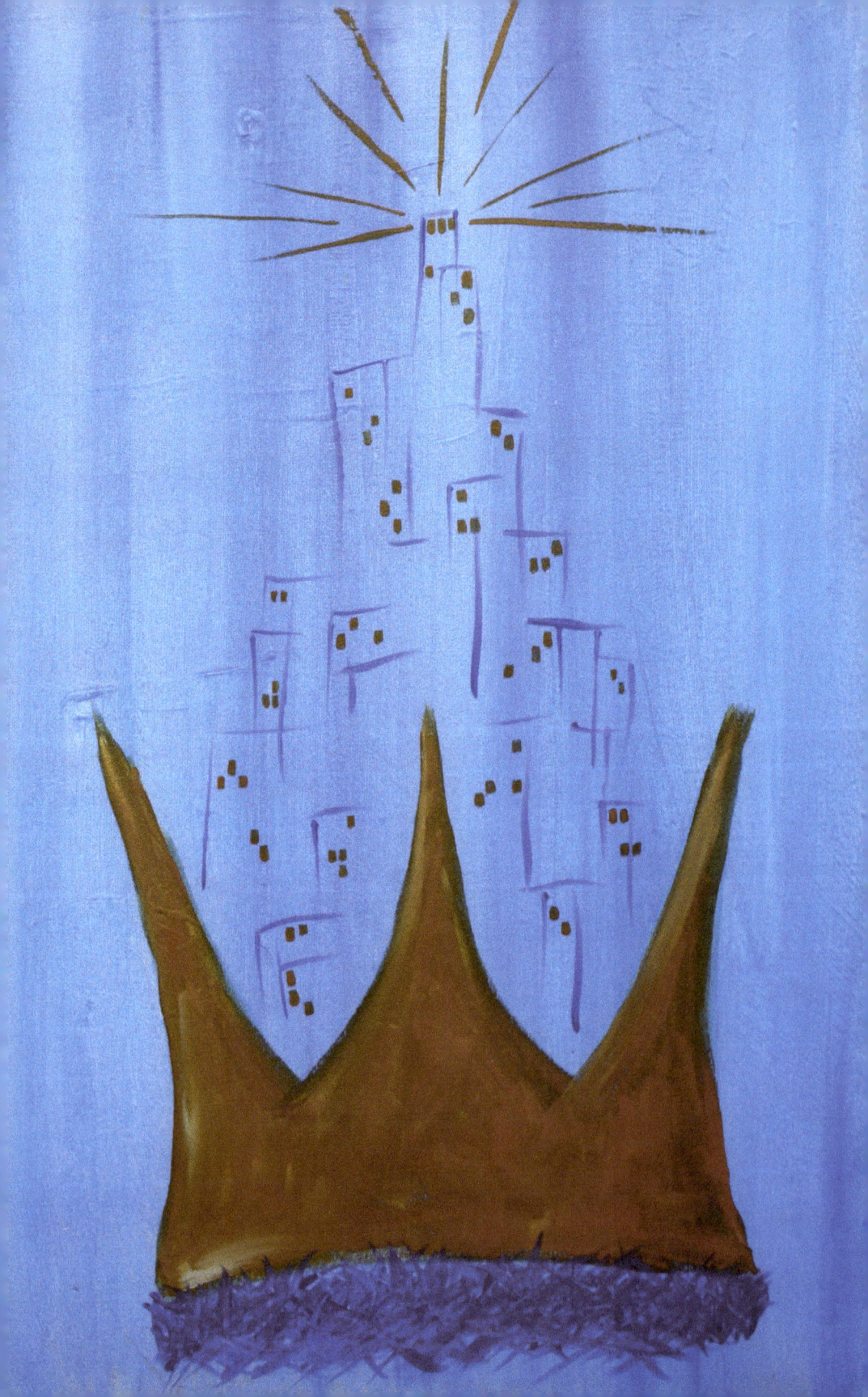

```
Ellie
```

Our Ellie is a genius.
We're certain this is true.
She knows the whole long alphabet,
And sums up two plus two.

Her shapes are always shapely,
In yellow, red, and blue.
And when you give the answer,
She'll tell you that she knew!

```
Regroup
```

I have ten fingers and ten toes
Which I could count on
If sandals were allowed at school
This isn't working out so well
Time to regroup

Legacy

This is my legacy
I am not the trunk
But a recent branch
On a lofty limb
My children
Spring shoots
Nourished by words
In poetic veins
Drawn through
A thousand years
Of old growth
Producing soul fruit
Nourishing happy seed
To grow
Family trees

Loving

I look you in the eyes.
I hold you in my arms.
We talk about weather,
Stinky feet, and car alarms.

You don't know I love you
Cause I ran out of time.
I see how you wander
Without reason, without rhyme.

So I'll take this moment.
I'm giving it to you.
You don't understand love
From other points of view.

You know when I hold you.
You look into my face.
Your mommy really cares.
This is your loving place.

Growing

You used to lay upon my chest
And rise and fall with every breath.
Now you're cuddled next to me
Head at my ear, foot by knee.
Your dad feels rather put upon
I'm just glad you haven't gone.

Dangerous Dimples

A dimple is the devil's work,
No harmless little facial quirk.
It led my baby girl astray
Cause she could always get her way.

"I don't need your money, Mom,"
She drops another info bomb.
Explaining for me, in her case,
"I can buy things with my face!"

Le Salon

Short hair
Long hair
Fancy up and down chair
Funny sink
Smelly stink
Stuff that turns your hair pink
In with pout
Pretty out
Makes me want to dance about!

It's Staggering

I fling out my arms on the dance floor
And whirl my whole self around
I fly in this moment of faster and more,
Until I come crashing down

```
When Abby Goes A-Dancin'
```

The room's alive and spirit's alight
When Abby goes a-dancin'
A whirlin' twirlin' thru the night
When Abby goes dancin' away

The music's loud and drums are tight
When Abby goes a-dancin'
She'll make you smile and feel alright
When Abby goes dancin' away

Her hair is gold, her dress is white
When Abby goes a-dancin'
Puts you in mind of a lovely kite
When Abby goes dancin' away

Though some say she's a little mite
When Abby goes a-dancin'
You've never seen so fine a sight
When Abby goes dancin' away

It's poetry I could not write
When Abby goes a-dancin'
She must be tired but she's not quite
When Abby goes dancin' away

Daddy's Lap

We are three sisters who like to fight.
We all want Daddy's lap tonight!
We're watching a movie we love to see,
And we'd be cozy as can be,
If Daddy's lap, instead of one,
Could fit three girls to set upon.

We all want to cuddle, but it's hard to begin,
When Ellie and Maggie don't fit in.
Ellie is batting her eyelashes sweetly,
She edges out Abby, ever so neatly.
Then Maggie raises her voice in a fuss,
And climbs the mountain that's all of us.

Soon Abby's feet connect with a chin.
Dad can't hear his movie over the din.
So up he gets, from under us girls,
Brushes us off and moves with a whirl.
Then settles down in a comfy love seat,
With room for three girls to sit and be sweet!

My Baby

You'll always be my baby
No matter how big you get
You're the last at everything
And it frustrates you I bet

Your clothes are rarely new
The games have all been played
Your furniture is writ upon
And bedding's kinda frayed

When at last you started school
I didn't go home and cry
I couldn't help but celebrate
The last of my small fry

Your siblings are all jealous
They think you've got it best
You never work as hard, they say
You also never rest

I see how you push yourself
To keep up with their games
How they tease and badger you
And even call you names

You're the toughest kid I have
You always power through
You grunt and yell and laugh as well
And do what you must do

You'll always be the younger one
There's no way that will change
They broke your parents in for you
So it's true, we're slightly strange

When I see you graduate
I'll surely dance a jig
I'll throw a massive party
And cook the fatted pig

I hope that you won't take this wrong
I don't mean to offend
I'll give all of my best for you
Right to the very end.

Mom Jeans

We would wear them on a plane.
We would wear them in the rain.
Yes, we love our brand new jeans
Because we are Domestic Queens!

Just Like You

"Someday you'll have a kid like you,"
My mother used to say.
"And then you'll suffer like I do
Every single bloody day."

My mom was absolutely wrong
You'll all be glad to hear.
Instead I have this horrid child
Just like Mother dear.

Flea Bit

I thought that I had four children.
In fact, I was certain of it.
But I've only three,
And a puppy, see?
Who is quite terribly flea bit.

Oh Litterbox

Oh Litterbox, oh Litterbox
You smell much worse than dirty socks
Oh Litterbox, oh Litterbox,
You're so much worse than dirty socks
That poopy smear in underwear
Is better than the air in here
Oh Litterbox, oh Litterbox
I'd rather smell some dirty socks.

Ode to Fluffy

Ye present and possessive
Sentient furnishing
Of the house of spinsters
Ye apparition
In the house of children
Nimble and silent at will
Or teacher of tidiness
By destruction
Insistent little yogini
Be at peace
Connect
Purr
Valiant defender
Against pest and plague
Giving comfort
Needing nothing
Woman's best friend

'R's

'R's are very hard to say.
I try to keep those 'R's at bay.
They creep in where they shouldn't
'Cause they're terribly imprudent
So I sound like a pirate, Yay!

Making Sense

I have two ears, two eyes, one nose
One tongue, and all this skin.
Five senses
That can tell me everything
I want to know,
But when to shut up.

Homecoming

The sun sets in a rosy glow
That, almost, rivals your smile.
Night wraps warmth around us like the
Velvet skimming your shoulders.
The sparkles on your dress,
And in your eyes,
And on all the accoutrements of a
Girl's first high school dance.
They're blinding me.
That's what's causing these tears.
They call it Homecoming,
But you're leaving me
A little more
Each day.

Yo' Momma

I can't write angry political crap.

I can't cuss and I can't rap.

I write rhymes that
make your momma cry,

'Cause her poor boy was just like my

Four darling daughters.

When you peed your
Transformers sheets,

Did you ever think she'd be
sentimental

For the boy that needed her.

That greeted her with hugs, and
kisses, and smiles,

Never knowing when they'd turn
to denials.

'Cause you grew into those
big boy pants,

And you come here with your
pitiful rants

Thinkin' you know what it is
to suffer.

But you don't know what it is for her

To grow an extra body, and watch it

Walk away under its own power.

While she still feels every twinge
and every touch

Because what you think is
only yours

Is her phantom limb,
thank you very much.

When you get two, three, four

Of those things walkin' around,

Too stupid to avoid the same holes
you stumbled in,

You might sympathize.

Write your momma a ballad.

An homage to clean sheets in
your clever beats

And a love you couldn't comprehend

When love was just about what girl

You'd end up living your life for.

And you think she's the hot chick

Eyeing your prick from across
the bar.

But she's still the twinkle in your eye

The girl you'll live and die,
and slave away

Eight hours a day

At your sucky job for,

Year in and year out

'Cause she meets you at
the front door with a shout

Of "Daddy!"

Then you'll take my little book

Of childhood memories in verse,

And read it before bedtime
every night.

'Cause your babies look

Like cherubs when they sleep,

And eight lines are all I need

To make you cry.

Runaway

I'd like to run away
See the world for myself
Walk a quiet byway
Find the continental shelf

I'd like to hear the howling
Of wind across a plain
Terrifying thunderclaps
Roar of coming rain

Not the whine of tiny tots
Or the splatter of a spill
I've got to get outta here
And, one day, I will

I'll drive on every highway
Never getting "there"
Stop because I want to
And go without a "where?"

I'll smile at the sunshine
Laugh at weather foul
I've none but me to care for
And I brought myself a towel

When I stop to chat with cacti
They will tell me of their days
How they gossip with the insects
While soaking up the rays

When I swim with little fishes
They'll perform for me ballet
When I come across a person
I will try to sneak away

Rainbows are for chasing
Bridges are to cross
Oceans are for sailing
(Cookies are to toss!)

I want to learn to fly
Navigate the air
Then jump out of my plane
To make the birdies stare

I could climb a mountain
Just to say that I have done
Of course, I'll go back home
When there's nowhere left to run.

To be

Who I am
In the Light.

To see
What I can
Through Your eyes.

To live
Just to be
In Your Heart.

To know
That You see
As I am.

```
Wanted:
```

Eclectic furnishings
For a palatial mind
Shop the world over
Treasure what you find

```
With This Pen...
```

The line, the flourish, the flow...
The heft, the texture, the tone...
Union that can't be undone...
Reason for me to write on...

An American Woman

The daughter of thousands
Of generations of survivors,
Of nomads and farmers,
Of queens and warriors,
Of colonists and rebels,
Of pioneers and settlers,
Of activists and actionists.
You possess your own brain,
Your body, a voice, and a vote.
You have the freedom
To do anything, and be anything,
You are willing to work hard to do,
And to be.
You are powerful.

```
Ok Woman
```

Time to shut it down
We both know you're brilliant
But I've got you
Naked in my bed
Time to turn into the blonde bimbo
That shags me senseless

Yes Dear (keeps writing)

Snore...

The (Self) Critique

I didn't like it.
It was sipping through a straw when I wanted to do a keg stand.
It was flowers and trees and metaphors when I wanted an orgasm,
        hard and fast and maybe in a dark alley with a stranger.
Okay, maybe not.
It was just so very long and drawn out that I lost interest,
        rolled over and fell asleep.
Please, can we get this over with.
When a photograph could replace your thousand words,
        you should let it.
When your book feels like a slide show of your vacation
Bury it in the garage with the projector.
A criminal waste of words has been committed.
The victims lie unconscious in a pool of sickly sweet syrup
        laced with cat hairs.
Get a hose.
We've been too kind.
In MFAs and AAs and 3rd grades we've encouraged the writing
        of self indulgent therapeutic shite
Which is neither amusing
Nor ennobling
Nor disruptive to the comfortable peace inside our heads,
For there's certainly no peace outside.
Try again.

In Celebration of a Locked Door

Thrum of bodies in harmony
Primal dance of thrust and soar
Nerves singing opera to the heavens
One heart in two bodies
Demanding, no, pleading for rejoining
Finding peace in passion
Satisfaction in want
Completion in breaking
Heavenly consolation for a curse
What luxury is a locked door!

Electroshock Therapy

Your face is sunshine
You may be plain, average, unexceptional
But I can't see it
I am blinded by the light you bring
Into my ordinary day at a time existence
Making life a thing to anticipate

Exhaling tension at first touch
I melt into you
Your lips, your hands
Hot roving points of contact
In an electrical storm
Electroshock therapy of the best sort

About the Author

    E.A.Provost is one of the millions of Elisabeths in the world, hiding behind a plethora of abbreviations and nicknames. She started life in Petersburg, Alaska, but spent the majority of it in Sonoma County, California where she now lives with her husband, four daughters, and six cats. In between PTA meetings, grocery shopping, and kids doctor appointments, she writes poetry, science fiction, and overlong facebook posts. Her house is as messy as you might imagine in light of that information. In addition to this volume, she has published a poetry chapbook called *Love, Joy, & Pees* because new parents have more misplaced urine in their lives than peace. You can find her other books and ramblings on the web at www.themensamom.blogspot.com.

Appendix

The Dark Side:

Introduction	1
Resilience in the Redwoods	2
I can't feel your pain	3
Burn for Me	4
We didn't evolve for comfort	5
Light from the Roots	6
Identity	6
On Witnessing my own descent into depression	7
Revelation of Life	8
First World Poverty	8
Deeper	10
My Kayak	11
Canary Solitaire	12
What a Hand Weighs	13
Lovers	13
Oak on Fire	14
Summer of Love	15
JC+Me	16
I feel nothing	16
Passion	17
I'm Sending You Flowers	18
Time of Death	19
Sonrise	20
Life Instructions:	21
The Border Between States	22
Shot	22
Grieve Not	23
Alone with God	24
To the Baby Boomers	24
Overflowing	26
Get Understanding	27
Tears of Heaven	28
Lost	28
I am	29
Aurora	30
December	31
Flux	31
The Meeting Place	32
Avoiding the Abyss	33
Wedding Cake	34
In Celebration of a Locked Door	35
Electroshock Therapy	35
Sunspots	36
The (Self) Critique	37
Okay Woman	38
All Together	39
About the Author	40
Appendix	41

Appendix

The Light Side:

Introduction 1
Surfing a Tsunami of Revelation 2
Superstorm Winnie 3
Tree of Life 4
When You Were Small 5
Revelation of the Meek 6
The Dawdler 6
I Promise 6
Perspective 6
Optimistic Child 7
The Sovereign Bubble 8
The Smart Kids' Excuse 9
City of the Great King 10
Ellie 11
Regroup 11
The Meadow 12
Legacy 12
Loving 13
Growing 13
Fill My Cup 14
Dangerous Dimples 15
Le Salon 15
Abby Dancing 16
It's Staggering 16
When Abby Goes A-Dancin' 17
The Bride 18
Daddy's Lap 19
My Baby 20
Gravity 21
The Happy Home 22
Mom Jeans 22
Just Like You 23
Flea Bit 23
Coffee Filters 24
Oh Litterbox 24
Ode to Fluffy 25
The Gifts Flow Together 26
'R's 27
Making Sense 27
Life Overcoming 28
Homecoming 29
Nativity 30
Yo' Momma 31
Shuttle Landing 32
Runaway 33
The Church 34
To be 35
Galaxies 36
Wanted: 37
With This Pen… 37
American Woman 38
Appendix 39

Avoiding the Abyss

Deep is for other days
When focus wanders like
an errant cloud
And peers on quiet scenes
of life or death
And heads bowed in a
silent prayer
For hope restored and grace
To be poured out in the
place where hearts break
Over stones that will not
be moved
By the hands of men.

Deep is for other days
When the pinpoint of my
existence
Cannot restrain my soul
Casting off resistance
Taking flight beyond the sky
Into the night, where I set down
Feet on planets only theorized
By crazy math guys in a town
Nobody cares to mention
'Til they disintegrate
convention.

Deep is for other days
When the tensile strength
of an idea
Tested by sleeper waves.
Currents and pressure
Slaves of physics and media
In an ocean of what is possible
But mostly not gonna
happen anyway.
Six ways to spend a life well
But I've only one to pay.
Could I sell you another?

Today my thoughts take refuge
In a two hour lifeboat called
romantic comedy
Forty four ounce coca cola
remedy
For over thinking everything.
Floating in caffeine bliss
I borrow the musings of a
lighter mind.
Could I miss the kind of thoughts
That drag me to perilous depths
Where I conceive the future?
Not today.

```
December
```

There are a million things to say

And I am mute

The tree is in the window

But the decorations remain in the attic

I am well it seems

Though by all appearances I am sick

Heart heavy, mind spinning,

Pocket empty, life full

Another day is coming on

I hold myself together

The days slow down

Or speed up

Taking me to when

And where

I am who I ought to be

```
                                        Flux
```

Oh miserable morning,

Sleepwalking,

Pretending,

Drifting to a distant shore

Where lies the comfort of darkness again.

A day closer

To the next scheduled engagement

With the world outside,

The next moment of change,

The tension putting me to sleep.

`I am`

Pressing in...
I am formed about you.
Taking the shape
Of your body onto mine.

Seeing dimly in glass
Your reflection.
Taking your image
For my own.

Standing confidently
In your cover.
Here I am,
Where I cannot be seen.

Tears of Heaven

The tears of Heaven are
Tears that flow down my face.
Compassion moves me to
Hold dear what You embrace.

Lost

You may feel lost, but it won't come to that.
Hope is going forth from where I'm at.

Get Understanding

A strong opinion so often leads astray.
Be fixed on none.
But lash thyself in the crow's nest
Where all is observed,
And it takes a mighty effort to convey
The fewest words.
That only what's important
Will be ventured.

Let this truth be shouted from the height;
Iceberg! or Land ho!
What more is needed? Measurements?
Descriptors?
We are either dying, or are saved.
Thumbs and stars
And well crafted five paragraph essays,
With citations,

Change nothing that is elemental.
Arguments sink
Beneath the weight of experience.
That rushing
Boisterous sea we navigate together, yet
Feel ourselves alone
Because we try to convince, instead of
Understand.

Reinforced our economy
With lies,
Went to bed with
Our enemies,
Racked up debt
On our credit.
We survive.
When we bore children
You asked, "Why"?
Don't you know
What kind of world
You're bringing them into?
Autism, Cancer, Diabetes, AIDS,
Terrorism, Jihad,
Unemployment, Homelessness,
Revolution, Climate Change.
Your legacy.

Our dubious inheritance.
We know.
We will Survive.
What of our legacy?
Communication,
Innovation,
Revelation.
Renovation
By the fire
Of our determination.
We forge a new world
So our children
Will not wonder why.
We fight for truth.
Sacrifice for stability.
Give them identity.
For this purpose.
When we have all succumbed,
They may Thrive.

```
To the Baby Boomers;
```

Twenty five percent
Of my generation
Never made it
Out of the womb alive.
You made our existence
A matter of your choice.
So maybe our opinions differ
About abortion.
About a lot of things.
You couldn't wipe us out,
So you stamped us
With an X.
We reject your label.
We are not anonymous.
We are Survivors.
You thought marriage
Was about you,
About what you want,
About your feelings.
You denied us
The safety and stability
Of a united home.
Our feelings didn't matter
You called us reckless,
Irresponsible.
It was your recklessness,
Your irresponsibility,
We Survived.
You poisoned our food,
And our water,
And our air,
For your profits.
You experimented
With our education,
Bought and sold
Our representative government,

```
Grieve Not
```

If life ends in immortality
grieve not.
If termination is oblivion
the same.
You cannot take one particle
beyond.
Cognition may alone be what
we save.

Neither will benefit
the living.
The fear of death will never
profit me.
Let my mind be free to roam
the vapor;
While my ashes vanish
in the sea.

Shot

I'm broken and I'm dying
Abandoning the pieces
I stagger outside
Air flows through me
I take up no space
Not really here
Beginning to drift
Learning to fly

Life Instructions: Upon Completion

Dying takes too long

Let me go quickly

No lingering treatment

Praying for another month

Another week

Another day

That this pill holds off death

Until another is approved

Watching loved ones slip

Slowly

Inexorably

Into poverty

For the privilege of grieving a zombie

Another month

Another week

Another day

That will end as surely

And painfully

As if seized by the heart

Gone in an instant

Go quickly

Dying takes too long

Let me be dead

Time of Death

A wife weeping in the ICU
The soundtrack for CPR.
A violent last ditch effort.
The doctor persists, waiting.
Watching her frantic phone calls.
Reaching out for anybody.
A two a.m. connection,
So she won't be alone
When he calls time of death.
His patient is beyond saving.
But the CPR
Keeps another heart beating,
Until a friend arrives.
An emotional pacemaker,
Forcing her heart to beat
When it is broken
Beyond his ability
To make repairs.

Passion

Lost in Your passion.
A thousand kisses
On my eyes tonight.
Where have I just gone?
Wrapped up in Your might.

Found in desperation.
My beloved seeks
In dark and desolate
Places, where I hide
My shame this night.

Another transformation.
I am lovely
In Your eyes and mine.
When did I become
Queen, and Your delight?

Summer of Love

I'm lying in bed with you;
Your hand on my naked thigh
You sleep deeply, sated

I'm jealous

40 hours a week
Your daily labor of love
It takes so little recompense

To satisfy

Head aching from
Twisted contemplations
Turning labor into life for you

Like magic

Guilt and gratitude
To be myself but never selfish
Failing in my own eyes but,

You're blind

Take all and be happy
Then I will be content and cry, "Success!"
My responsibility, my achievement

My love

In the long hard summer of life

```
What a Hand Weighs
```

What does a hand weigh
Not much, surely
Yet the pressure
Of your palm
In sleep
Is the burden of possession
An imprint seared
On living skin
A fastening between souls
A channel of flesh
Through which may flow
Passion words cannot express
Truths too intimate for eyes
Unconscious touch
Leave your hand
Forever
On my side

```
                Lovers
```

Some lovers inflate
From all their hot air.
Others are timid
But always aware.

Some lovers are brash
Courageous and bold.
But the best lovers
Aren't young, they are old.

The greatest lovers,
Whose sagas linger,
Count all their conquests
On one small finger.

My Kayak

What can I say that will not be lost
In the ocean of what has already been said?
My words glide like a kayak
Skimming the surface of deep thoughts.
I peer over the edge, into the abyss,
Only to see my reflection.
I plumb the depths with great intent
To measure what I do not know.
But I cannot know it from the surface.
I give myself up to knowledge.
Sacrifice the sun and the stars
To bury myself in the deep.
Embrace the cold, the dark, and the pressure
Where I cannot breathe
To know what other men have learned.
If I play in the shallows like a child
I may be wiser
Than to sacrifice too much of life for knowledge.
But I will always long to go deeper.

on the dance floor.
It whispers in my ear
In the soft tones of affection
How it will kill me
If I stumble.
It seems it should be so simple.
I know the steps.
But it never is.
Dancing with a devil.
Holding him at a distance.
Refusing to sell my soul
To buy bread.
I envy the gold digger.
Money can't buy happiness.
But I know how to be happy.
I don't know how to live without money.
So, I think longingly of death.
And I write.

First World Poverty

When there is no money,
I want to hide my head in a hole.
The papers I must deal with pile up.
What can I do?
We live well enough
But I don't know how.
Credit grips me too tightly
In a slow spiraling dance of debt.
I am overcome by a chill
That cripples my will to act.
Food, clothing, and shelter
Make life seem alright
Until someone gets sick.
There is pride in a paycheck
Until a holiday comes
And a day is lost.
Another bill goes unpaid.
Credit pulls me a little closer

```
On witnessing my own
    descent into depression.
```

It's not me.
    I'm not me.
I don't know where I went
But this can't be me.

It's not me.
    I'm not me.
I can throw this self away,
So, I can't be me.

It's not me.
    I'm not me.
This isn't how I end,
Alone, without me.

It's not me.
    I'm not me.
I looked within myself
But I was gone.

The piece of me you carry,
    That you nurture in your chest,
Will be the me that finds me,
When none of me is left.

Identity

Do I know me?
Is this flesh a place
I want to be?
Is my spirit bound
Or does it fly free?

We didn't evolve for comfort

Struggle is our purpose
Joy and pain exist only
As relative states
My status for today
Because yesterday was better
Or others have it worse
Because someone did or didn't
It's not fair, Life's not fair
We use all these words
That mean nothing
To make us feel upright
In a vast directionless universe
X, Y, Z axis all in a tumble
With jumbled up ideas about
Ways and means to ease
And nothing means anything
Apart from trying again tomorrow

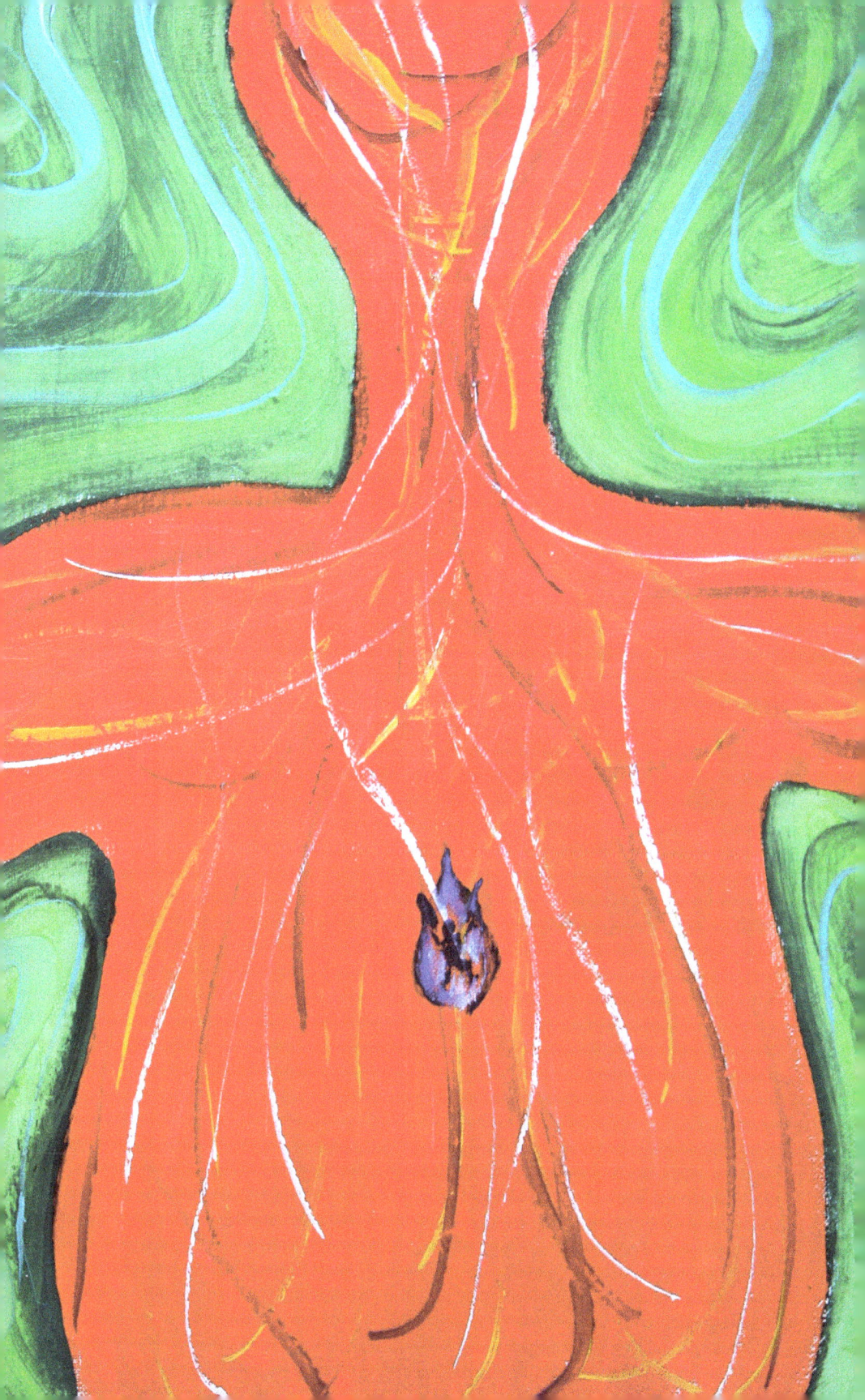

I can't feel your pain.

I won't feel your pain.
I've felt the unending
Anguish of a million
Deaths paraded in garish
Light before rapt eyes
Until my soul bled a
River of all the fucks
I ever had to give,
And I'm empty now.
A porcelain shell
With glass eyes that
Don't flinch, and don't
Cry, and pretty lips that
Don't sigh and breathe
Platitudes to comfort
Those who haven't
Learned that life is not
What you gather, but
A long, hard race
To lose it all.
My pain is enough.
To think of seven billion others
Suffering in solidarity
Is enough.
I cannot feel it all
And survive.

Hi, I'm Lissa.
I'm weird.

The word "Poetry" means different things to different people. For some, it's a set of rules that constrain and challenge us to elevate our language. For others, it's a liberation of language from the constraints of grammar. For some, it's a layering and twisting of meaning to communicate more deeply. For others, it's a medium free of any obligation to communicate, an arrangement of words and sounds that give pleasure without meaning. Some write from the beginning with an ear for performance, while others write in a way that is only fully appreciable in print.

Such oppositional viewpoints are completely acceptable within the community of poets. There is a universal acknowledgement that creating an engaging work of poetry is extremely difficult, and appreciation of the product is entirely subjective. Its beauty is in the ear of the listener. All of us feel the challenge of our craft perpetually. There is no moment where we "arrive" as poets and are suddenly capable of cranking out magnificient poems one after another. Thus, publishing a book of poetry is a gut wrenching task.

You may love one of my poems and hate another. I'd be quite happy with both reactions. For me, poetry is about connection and we connect when we elicit emotional reactions. The light direction of this book is meant to make you smile. The poems you now face in the dark direction may make you angry or sad. They include poems of lonliness and pain.

When I was 13 I decided to take my introverted agonized self, accept it, and force a personality shift that would enable me to be the extroverted person I wanted to be. I started introducing myself, "Hi, I'm Lissa. I'm weird," and whenever I was afraid, I did the thing I feared. I succeeded in changing my personality. Every personality test I take puts me squarely in the center of the results. I can enjoy being extroverted and introverted. I can also suffer the pains of both.

Like so many other creative people, I've suffered from depression, and wondered if I might be bipolar. It's connection that pulled me back from the brink. It's exposure to the light of unrelenting love, that wilts the weeds of depression sprouting in our minds. If I hadn't habituated myself to doing things I fear from my teen years, I wouldn't have reached out for connection, I wouldn't be here today, and these poems would remain in the dark.

```
For Aaron
```

Why are you reading this? Because it looks all commerically printed? Can't you tell it's someone's DIARY?! It's copyrighted and everything! You should put it down right now before they catch you.

Diary
of that
Weird Girl

Warning: Adult Content

www.ingramcontent.com/pod-product-compliance
Lightning Source LLC
Chambersburg PA
CBHW042227010526
44113CB00043B/2709